MORE AMERICAN

MORE AMERICAN

poems by Sharon Hashimoto

Off the Grid Press

Published by:
Grid Books
Boston, Massachusetts
grid-books.org

Cover painting: "Kin Narita" (detail), by Alan Lau.
Printed by Cushing–Malloy, Inc., Ann Arbor, Michigan.
Book design by Michael Alpert.

ISBN 978-1-946830-10-4

ACKNOWLEDGMENTS

For their friendship, support, and feedback, I am grateful to John Davis, Susan Landgraf, Robert McNamara, Sati Mookherjee, Arlene Naganawa, Ann Spiers and John Willson. Special thanks to Lonny Kaneko (1939–2017)—with whom many of these poems began in a poetry correspondence—and to Alan Lau for his artistic and poetic generosity. Lastly, my greatest appreciation to Michael Spence for loving the sounds and imagery, and sharing his poetic inspirations.

Asian Pacific American Journal: "What My Blind Grandfather Showed Me"; *Barrow Street:* "Day of Departure"; *Blue Lyra Review:* "On Hearing of a Friend's Onset of Alzheimer's"; *Colere:* "One of the World's Oldest Twins Dies at Age 107 in Japan: Kin Narita, 1892-2000"; *Connecticut Poetry Journal:* "Midnight, Listening to the Spotted Hound Seen Wandering Through the Kobashi's Farm"; *Crab Creek Review:* "Kokusai Theatre, Seattle, 1965"; *Crosscurrents:* "Submerged Clothesline, Salton Sea, 1983"; *Diner:* "Color Snapshot, Oregon Coast, 1972," and "Argument on the Beach, Vashon Island"; *Enizagam:* "First Chinese Brother: Swallowing the Sea," "Steelhead Fishing," and "Hard Shell Clamming"; *Footbridge Above the Falls* (Rose Alley Press): "A Bus Driver's Wife," "A Barrack's Window, Inside," "A Barrack's Window, Outside," and "Those Left to Tell: For A.C."; *Fourth River:* "Nuclear Cattle"; *Kettle Blue:* "Seven Haiku from My Grandmother at the Kawabe House"; *Louisiana Literature:* "At the Richard Hugo House"; *North American Review:* "A Matter of Loyalty: Question #28, A Nisei's Response," "Soft," "To Erlinda: Fifty Years Later," and "The Bus Driver's Wife"; *One:* "The Feral Cats"; *PONTOON:* "In Hawai'i, We Do This"; *Raven Chronicles:* "The Guest Bedroom"; *The Same:* "Those Left to Tell," "Theodor Jacobsen Observatory," and "The Golfer's; Daughter"; *Seattle Woman:* "Sciurus Griesus"; *Sextant Review:* "August 9th"; *Shenandoah:* "Mangoes"; *South Dakota Review:* "Oriental Flavors"; *Sow's Ear:* "My Grandmother Peeling Onions"

For my parents

Tokiko "Karen" Hashimoto
November 1, 1924 to November 21, 2005

and

John Isamu Hashimoto
March 20, 1922 to February 25, 2016

TABLE OF CONTENTS

MORE AMERICAN

PART I: JAPANESE-AMERICAN DICTIONARY

ORIENTAL FLAVORS

Cookbook published by St. Peter's Sunday School
September 1952 (5th printing)
1610 King Street
Seattle 44, Washington

My grandma didn't have a measuring spoon
or cup. Dinner began with headless birds
that sprinted till they dropped. Pulling pinion
feathers, she broke the bodies open, gizzards

steaming with their own warmth, each recipe
a mimeograph blurred with Mom's
blue notations. Worked into shoyu-soaked ropes,
chicken sizzled in garlic and fat. Home

was smell: seaweed, ginger, and rice wine
vinegar. I grind sesame seeds, pestle
in Grandma's suribachi. Noodles soften
in the roiling pot. The book begins to fall

apart beneath my fingers. I search for the way
Grandma stuffed rice into wrinkled skins of age. *

*deep fried bean cake

MY GRANDMOTHER PEELING ONIONS, 1934

In the moment between reaching
for another dirt-stained onion, she leans
her elbows on the kitchen table.
The sharp smell clings to everything she touches:
wooden boxes, loose earth, burlap,
the bibbed apron tied behind her back.
She rubs one eye with the upper sleeve
of her cotton dress, then cleans membrane
and clipped roots from the paring knife
blade. Inside the dry shed, behind
the house, rows of rough woven bags
bottom out like Buddhas. She tallies
the numbers in her head. Two dollars
for a ton of burlap; two dollars twenty-five cents
for the same weight of onions. Flexing
her fingers, she reaches for another globe
to balance in the palm of her hand.

MIDNIGHT, THE SPOTTED HOUND WANDERS THROUGH THE KOBASHI'S FARM

The triangle of his head cocked,
some strange sound catches
his ear, triggers the far-off call
to something not yet lost
in his blood. Listening, he lowers
his jaw to the earth, then releases
the deep bell of his throat.
Again, his voice pursues the ravine,
but the open night closes in
faster. Crouched down on his belly,
with his eyes closed, he can feel
the furrowed land like the echoes
of his howl ringing
the moon.

FIRST CHINESE BROTHER: SWALLOWING THE SEA

after Claire Huchet Bishop

I.
Bowing at the edge, I can feel
the grainy sand beneath my palms.
I name the waters, lower my chin.
I unhinge my jaw to take everything in.
The first taste is a sip of foam—everything
the village boy doesn't know,
his finger poking clam holes
to force a high-arc squirt.
He stands, hands fisted at his sides,
as each level is revealed:
barnacles, anemones, bronzed
and many-legged starfish. My tongue
is a wave in my mouth, rushing
and flowing—kelp and jellyfish
like the blood I hold in the chambers
of my heart. When I close
lips over the last dregs, my cheeks
bulge with fullness, with roiling.
I am indigo, azure, aquamarine.

II.
Sun dims the scales of deep-sea fish
flopping their tails, gills puffing in and out.
I never thought the world could be
this quiet without the ebb and flow
of tides. Far from shore, the village boy

zigzags towards a cast-off anchor,
to a tangled octopus, towards a sucking
rivulet. Shoes crushing shells—
such a small sound. Something
rises and curls inside me: wanting out.
I raise five fingers as if I could draw the boy back.
I drum a driftwood branch
against a wide log. I flag my shirt
into the wind. His small shape
wanders further. Perhaps like
so many young, he chooses not to see.
Sweat breaks out under my chin.
I sputter. When the dam of my lips
finally parts, the sea spews forth.
My voice is lost in the sea's own,
the boy's last words as loud,
as raucous as a seagull's two-note cry.

KOKUSAI THEATRE, SEATTLE, 1965

I.
The aisle slants downward. In the dark,
I could be sliding into the big movie screen
where men with bushy eyebrows grunt,
wearing kimonos like the women
who clack their sandals with quick short steps,
hiding hands in their sleeves. Tea pours
into cups too small to hold. The husband speaks.
His wife looks into her lap. The son's voice
trembles. I think how everything is fragile
in a rice paper house.

II.
Reading the English subtitles,
the words don't match what we see.
When the mother kneels beside the sleeping
quilts to touch her boy's face,
what she says isn't "darling."

III.
The story grows sadder and sadder.
When the boy kneels beside his mother's futon,
her breathing slows, stops—eyes never opening
to see him. Suddenly the theatre fills with weeping.

My grandmother's hand tightens
on my arm; she dabs her cheeks,
noisily blowing her nose. Around me

hunch the old ladies I've just met: Kato,
Matsudaira, cranky lady Fukuhara
who argues over the price of shoyu.
All are silhouetted in the dim light.

WHAT MY BLIND GRANDFATHER SHOWED ME

His big hands outstretched,
I believed those fingers could reshape shadows,
his open palms push away the night
as he reached for the chair's back,
the blunt blade of a table. Everything
was softer in moonlight. I didn't see
his eyes, only the tilt of his head
when he listened to the rug
brush against his bare feet.
Knowing I watched him, did he feel
my breath's thin release? Slowly, I let him
guide me over walls and edges, the cool handles
of the buffet. Exposed in the morning's harsh light,
I stood in a room surrounded by his touch.

JAPANESE-AMERICAN DICTIONARY

I.

The baby pulls himself up,
stubby fingers grasping
the playpen rails
to watch his mother push
the carpet sweeper back and forth
in front of the sofa, under
the coffee table. She laughs
at his wet-chin smile, his mouth
drooling, pursing with effort.
Gorogoro, she says
and he rumbles the sound
in his throat.

II.

She's afraid of the sliver,
the dark hyphen across her palm—
the flesh swollen and red.
But she's more afraid of the silver
needle, the point poised,
ready to dig. *Hold your hand
still,* her father tells her, *so we can
take it out.* She cries to make him
put the needle away; she cries
because she wants the sliver out.
Guzuguzu girl, he sighs.

COLOR SNAPSHOT, OREGON COAST, 1971

On a driftwood log bleached
smooth as a whale, my grandmother rides
side-saddle in her print housedress,
the heavy cardigan buttoned up
three from the bottom, sleeves neatly cuffed
around her wrists, hands clutching
the slippery wood. There's something
wild in the way she leans
as the wind hurls sand at her glasses,
teasing the scarf with its knot beneath her chin,
her bare feet wearing pale pink zoris.

SUBMERGED CLOTHESLINE, SALTON SEA, 1983

How easily the backyard slipped away,
green grass forgetting its shape going gray, then blue
the garden filling with water.
How the rudder-like gate moved in a tide
before sinking under. This slowness
wears down the husk of my skin—
the salty taste of my blood so like the sea.
I cannot touch my cheek and remember the feeling.
Water level rising up the narrow shafts,
how wide the arms of each wooden pole?
My hands are full of clouds I pin to the line.
Each sheet turns and thins out of existence.

NUCLEAR CATTLE
Fukushima, Japan

That day, I stood—knees locked—on my four feet
to stand my ground as it began to sway.
I didn't see but I smelled the change:
dirt littered with fallen swallows overwhelmed
by muddy ash. My herd wandered
through broken fences. Some lay
where they were tethered. Others died
with heads thrust through the holes
of the troughs, waiting to be fed.

On the dirt farm road, buses shuttled
our people away. Dogs, pigs, cats—
we were all left behind: only our voices
filled the air. Soon bodies lay
amid splintered boards and puddles.
Some of us survived on our own,
grazing the abandoned rice paddies.
We lifted our heads to bulldozers
and tractors hauling the dead

to burning pyres, inky columns
of smoke billowing in the wind.
Forty days later, my farmer came back.
The pastureland is overgrazed. Hungry,
I eat whatever feed he brings me
though white spots break out
along my flanks. With his Geiger counter

ticking, he strokes the place
between my ears.

AMEN

As I sat across from Grampa at the tablecloth
of red-and-white checkers, my fingers dusted
crumbs off the vinyl where I learned to place

a fork and spoon next to chopsticks on a napkin
folded into triangles. In my grandparents'
kitchen, I didn't know I was American

as the spit-curled hair of the Campbell Kids
salt and pepper shakers. I sipped my milk
from a Welch's jam glass. Grampa pointed

and smiled at the barrettes parting and holding
my bangs to each side. *High-tone*, he murmured
in his mangled English. I lifted my eyebrows,

imagining the phrase. Gramma shuffled her zoris
across linoleum, pushing up the sleeves of an orlon sweater,
throwing wood into a half-electric stove where a pot of rice

boiled. After fanning the flames to heat the cast-iron pan,
she added sliced rounds from a package
of hot dogs. Grampa puffed his pipe from behind

his newspaper, his nikkan shinbun. The kitchen filled
with the smell of St. Albert's and slightly charred beef.
Gramma's hands added sugar, ketchup, a swirl of shoyu.

Nothing tasted so good as sneaking bites
of raw egg on hot rice, the wienie mixture, and peeking at Gramma's
bowed head as she blessed our meal.

SOFT

Who could sleep that night,
at my grandmother's on a sofa
tucked into afghans
with crocheted coverings
that I used to pretend
were twirling skirts. When a ruler
of light leaked into the living room
where I lay, I crawled out
from the makeshift bed,
setting one bare foot after
the other on the brilliant balance
beam until I stood before
the bathroom and the vertical
slice of a barely open door.

Grandma was rising out of the steamy
bath, thin hair slicked smooth. Between
strands, I saw her scalp—white
as a peeled and boiled egg.
The broad stalk of her back bloomed
into buttocks, plump bags that hung over
her legs. When she turned,
breasts swung like socks stretched
as far as they could go. I stared
at the dark circles of her nipples
pointing out. As she stepped out
of the tub onto a mat, flesh rolled

escaping the water.

        But there was something
gentle about the way an old woman
patted the neck dry, rounding
the shoulder with a faded towel,
smoothing the tender spots
inside elbows, behind her knees.
Baby talc spotted her skin
as she rubbed the smell
over the mound of her belly.

In the mirror's light, I watched
Grandma hold those wrinkled fingers
high above her head, gathered around
a tube of flannel—how the nightgown
tumbled to her ankles, how the fabric
twirled around each small step.

ONE OF THE WORLD'S OLDEST TWINS
DIES AT AGE 107 IN JAPAN:
KIN NARITA, 1892–2000

Dear sister, whoever thought
we'd live this long—monkey brows
furrowed, the remnants of our hair wisping
around necks, tickling our ears.

First things we lose last, and I am forgetting
the names of all those children—your eleven,
my four girls, the dead husbands
whose photographs dangle

on the bedroom wall. Such men
wouldn't recognize us now. What's left
is our first steps toddling through the farm,
chickens broody on their nests, pungent

straw and manure, the egg shell
pulsing warm in fingers and palm.
I know the throb in the hollow
of your throat beat in rhythm with mine.

Someone knelt beside my wheelchair
told me you had the flu—
how you skipped breakfast, wanting
to sleep through the morning meal.

No egg on rice. Nothing was sadder
than this. A part of me doesn't know you've died.
My breath catches as if I'm a girl,
running, just out of reach of your hand.

SEVEN HAIKU FROM MY GRANDMOTHER
IN THE KAWABE HOUSE

for Sayoko Toda

Knock, knock on room door—
peeking through a keyhole, I
see another eye.

*****

Elder person's room—
everyone fascinated
with the poinsettia.

*****

Face after face stare
back. I shrug. My weak hearing
makes talking look odd.

*****

Lip licking around
me—people gossip, tasting
many distressed words.

*****

Autumn yellow leaves—
thin sun—only one sudden
night of wind. All gone.

*****

Early, I wake—cold.
The comforter escaped, not
staying on my back.

*****

Coins in our pockets
come and go, gains and losses—
a parallel line.

ASLEEP

At twilight, we lay limbs down
to rest, softly on cotton mattresses.
We yield to sleep with widened yawns

and breathing slows to ripples in the grass;
our blood, an ebb tide lapping shores.
Between an eyelid flick, we pass

to crow-dark cliffs and falling, or soar
from throats of calla lilies. If minds
believe, our flesh will trust the risk, the dare

of death. What leaves our lungs are islands—
whistling snores, gasps at worlds we bend.

TO ERLINDA: FIFTY YEARS LATER

Fourth grade? Fifth grade?
The principal didn't know
where to place your IQ. But backed
against the wall in a spelling bee, you firmly
went through "oxymoron" without pauses, knowing the rules:
say the word twice, before and after, or you're out.
Take care of Erlinda, Miss Redlinger
said to me, but you had no coat, no lunch,
no three cents for milk—only the thin blue sweater
and one dress you wore every day. I never knew
you were hungry. Who kept you scrubbed,
smelling of Clorox, your hair unevenly trimmed?

In a nasal voice, you mimicked your aunt who put a mop
and your muscles to work: *Not that way!*
Then you'd frown and mutter *little bitch*—words
I didn't understand. When straight-A Julie
shot her hand up, you glared at her curled hair
held back by barrettes. We were the other
two Asians—Japanese, Filipino—dark-skinned
and silent. You pushed your sweater sleeves up
past your elbows or fastened the chipped button,
bottom to top.

For a week, we shared *Of Mice and Men,*
you tapping your pencil, waiting for me
to flip the page so you could speed on to Lennie
and his mouse. Your forehead furrowed;

I didn't know how you could glance
at a paragraph and know Lennie would die.

Because you were tardy, then sick, I stopped saving
assignments for you and counting the days you were gone.
Absent from the photographs of our eight-page
yearbook, you were only there in the beginning.

PART II: THE WAR

AUGUST 9TH

After the flash
blasting flat the shoji screens, brush-stroked
cranes straining necks
disappeared into ash. Mothers
evaporated—children
floated on sides of buildings,
ghosts of minutes before.
Haloed light lingered,
illuminating the cleared miles between blue
jutting mountains and the horizon. Before the lovers'
kiss was complete,
lips barely brushed—one
mushroom cloud bloomed.
Negative and positive burns
outlined women's backs,
patterns of water lilies or chrysanthemums,
quotes inked on a scroll. Cries
ricocheted throughout the ruins.
Survivors stood, stuttering: *So much was
taken.* Children sat hunched under broken
umbrellas, rocking themselves.
Vertical studs in walls creaked.
Where would fireflies go?
X-rays couldn't find them.
Yanking on a barren branch, people discovered
zero blossoms left to fall.

DAY OF DEPARTURE: MAY 9, 1942

Twelve years old, she struggles with balance—
one arm dragging the folding chair
whose rusted seat flaps open, the other hand
grasping a suitcase. It's humid, so hot.
Beneath her winter coat, her best
blue-striped dress, the one with puffy sleeves,
itches. On this last day in Yakima, heat
grows from the ground into the pleats.

The blinds for windows are latched down.
When she boards the train, she trips
on bags and bodies. In that midnight dark, a group
of young voices sings "Don't Fence Me In"
until they tire. When she rises
from the folding chair, a bump in the track
jolts her footing. For miles now,
a stranger's leg has pressed into hers.
From his sweating suit, a man's stink spreads.

A BARRACK'S WINDOW, OUTSIDE
Minidoka

Not meant to last,
              the mean molding
is slats of wood
            set side by side
while tar-paper
            panels have peeled.
All nailed with nine
              quick strokes. Knotty
pine boards patrol
            the porch, protect
against glary
           glass-eyed glances.
Windows widen
            at the top. The wind
blows in brown bits
            of sagebrush, night's
ill-starred islands
           of indigo.
Outside, night owls
            might dream—observe
sunsets' slow
         sink into shadow.
Lanterns burn low.
             Guards call: *Lights out!*

A BARRACK'S WINDOW, INSIDE
Minidoka

Picture two girls—
                in Peter Pan collars,
bangs banging
                foreheads, bouncing
on cots. Chatty,
                chins cocked, they chant
jump-rope jingles,
                joining their hands.
Seventy summers
                swept by. Streaks
of gray grizzle
                these great-aunts.
Sister, what did
                we see? Sagebrush!
Barracks, blankets,
                pot-belly stove.
Same, same. Even now,
                you sneeze like me—
long sniff, then snort.
                Bathroom's stinky.
The desert—all dust—
                dammed Pa's mouth.
Thirsty. Tepid
                water in tin mugs.
Nothing was nice
                or clean. Nightfall—
black-haired babies

                              bawled all the time.
          Wind wiped away.
                        Now who is who?

A MATTER OF LOYALTY: QUESTION #27

Are you willing to serve in the armed forces of the United States
on combat duty, wherever ordered?

With a single light bulb
burning over a table sawed
from a crate, it's hard to read
this question. How can anyone
be *willing to serve* when guards—
those shadows in a tower—
warn us off, away from barbed
wire? Snakes slip under,
back and forth to either side.

While knotholes in barrack walls
let in dust, we stare at our one window
where the only lock we can open
is inside.
          To kill or be killed
by bullet or bayonet or bomb
in *combat duty*? Who can raise
a rifle, peer through the sight—
shoulder thumping at the recoil?
Who can burrow into blasted
terrain, fire a flamethrower
into a bunker *wherever ordered?*

Neighbors murmur. Bearing down
on the tarpaper roofs, the sun
warms the rooms with a black smell.

From day to night,
there are so many shades of sky.

A MATTER OF LOYALTY:
QUESTION #28, A NISEI'S RESPONSE

*Will you swear unqualified allegiance to the United States of America
and faithfully defend the United States from any and all attacks by foreign
or domestic forces, and forswear any form of allegiance to the Japanese
Emperor or any other foreign government, power, or organization?*

What I knew of Japan
was in my parents' faces:
okasan, ojisan—the baby sounds
I sometimes used for mother, father.
And the food I was fed: tea
was ocha, rice was gohan.
But all words became translations.
One family's sons were Monroe,
Lincoln, Taft. A girl I knew
was named America. Everyday use
made her Mary.
                    For grade school,
I faced the flag unfurled above
the teacher's desk. *Allegiance* was
to classmates in a circle clasping hands,
to rivers and mountains on a map
beginning outside the door.

As I grew, I pomaded my hair
into a pompadour. My feet tapped time
to swing. How could I not be
American, farming berries, driving a Ford?

It's hard to *faithfully defend* a nation
that brought me to camp. My grandfather's sword
and records, the family hid away.
Two suitcases hold onto what's left.
Behind barbed wire, we made the best
of nothing—shikata ga nai—
with rock gardens and wildflowers
from desert land. How do I *forswear*
the Emperor in whose land
I never lived? Even sunset
on sagebrush could be beautiful.
Japanese kanji in a haiku
describe lightning, a crow's
harsh cry. What part of myself
do I forswear?

LETTER TO MY FATHER
FROM HIS FRIEND OVERSEAS
AUGUST, 1944

Dear Isami,

Eh, bruddah. It been long time since you,
me, and crazy guy Clyde walk out
of old McKinley High. Member playin pool—
stick in hand, elbow in air, ball in side pocket—
on wall, how we see Uncle Sam? Eyebrows
all bushy white, pointin finger, "I Want You."

Good thing, Clyde bad eyes make him 4F.
Good thing, your mother say no, you too young.
Recruiter give me stink eye because I Japanese,
but I member 100th Battalion, "one puka puka."

First we think uniform with arm patch, stripe
make us look good. Here secret: Japanese small—
so small we wear girl clothes—blouses
cut down. Sometime we get special requisition.
Combat boot too big. Hilo guy wear size 2½ EEE.

Camp Shelby, Mississippi—meet all kine people.
Mainland boys call me "Buddahead"—but I no pig.
We Hawai'ians call them "katonk"—you know
coconut sound hittin ground. Sure, they get confuse.
I say: You go stay go. I go stay come.
He shake head, point finger that circle round

and round. Other explain: You go ahead and go
and I'll come later on. Bumbye, we get along.

An den we go Italy, but boat take long time—
zig zag around submarines. Berth five deep,
me on top. Everybody sick, sick.

No make fun. First time fightin, I get
chicken skin. German tank fire. Man next to me
go down—arms, legs, all twisted like—
blood all ovah throat. Pau. Gone—so fast.
Kay den, I say to self. But lots more.

Isami, this hard to say. Maybe you think
wassamattayou. Every day we watch high place
in broken building. We go face down in mud.
Lucky one carried out on stretcher. Try pretend.
Try not ask, "Today day I die?"

Stay home, Isami. This fo real. Your family
need you. No come, stay. Long as you can.

Your pal,
Tak

SMITHSONIAN
Natural Museum of American History,
A More Perfect Union: Japanese-Americans
and the U.S. Constitution

My walk is slow among the black-and-white
photographs, so many shots of the same landscape
with different names: Manzanar, Minidoka, Gila River.
The same pictures of the evacuation order nailed
to buildings and telephone poles. Too young
to have been sent there myself, I pass another portrait
then stop, and turn back. This one of men
in fedoras and overalls, sweatered mothers
in line with kids. Suddenly, *you're* there—
the teen-ager ladling chili into a bowl.
Have you been sent back to stand over
the steaming pot? A placard on the wall
behind you says "dinner is served cafeteria style
at the Heart Mountain Relocation Center."
This is you, who now tells me you don't
remember much except sagebrush and coal
for the pot-bellied stove. Hair edges
into your eyes and you tilt your head down.
Nothing matters but the stripes on cuff
and collar of the baseball jacket you wear.
Careful not to spill when you give back the bowl,
do you look at the face of the hand that takes it?

PART III: NO WRONG TURNINGS

MANGOES

My grandmother lifts the corners
of her mouth—a smile with no teeth;
open palms coaxing me to her side.
It's hot, the thick air sticky on skin.

I stay at my mother's side, fingers
busy pleating the hem of her skirt
where I can hide. There's Uncle Kazuo
and Dad. My brother isn't poking

at my mosquito bites, but joining in
with the many voices speaking
in pidgin about "dem cars."
Then Mom's hands rest on my shoulders,

pushing me away, telling me "be good."
Grandma leads me outside
to where Chinese doves politely bow
at our feet and a red cardinal

hops into a five-gallon glass jar, pecking
up feed. I skirt the shade of the mango tree,
tiptoeing past puddles of shattered fruit
where the fruit flies hover low

close to the ground. I don't like Hawai'i.
Running to the driveway, I see
our Chevrolet's tires churn with dust.
In the rear window, the three black heads

of my family disappear.
My zori slippers slap against my heels,
but no one looks back. Around me,
the sun's rays are the bars of a prison.

"Bumbye, they come home," Grandma calls.
"I give you mango, yes?" I don't understand
what she says about Uncle's car "no go,"
about a battery, or the two orange ovals

she cradles against her body. From her kitchen
door, I watch as she peels the skin,
slicing the fruit. All I know is that the juice
stings the small cuts in my mouth.

EXPECTATIONS

A boy should be born first—
not this swaddled girl who wanted
the dark, not opening her eyes

in these first weeks like a cat,
not gaining the weight of her percentile.
A boy should be born first.

He'd crawl on time, hands gripping the crib
to bounce on toes and yell for Ma.
What's in the dark? Not opening eyes

keeps the nursery blue with rocket ships.
A mother's arms cradle what she wanted:
the boy. Before, unborn, first

was the son in the womb who stopped
his slow turning like the quarter moon
in the dark, who never opened his eyes.

Mother, son. Mother, daughter. Nothing
can be planned for. No stars
for the boy who should be born first.
So dark. The girl-baby opens her eyes.

AT THE RICHARD HUGO HOUSE
February, 2012

Cold on a Sunday, in the creaky room,
we shift in our chairs
lining the three sides of a table.

An age spot rides a cheekbone.
His whiskered eyebrows shudder
as he follows an index finger, words

rushed and stumbling, sometimes misread.
Outside, a car alarm blares—the sound
switching on and off:

Iambic, the bags of his jowls sigh.
When sunlight strikes the back
of the old poet's head, he recites

from a younger memory, Margaret
who was grieving for goldenrod
unleaving. His voice grows

deep as rivers, our faces
reflected in the lens of the bifocals
hanging on the edge of his nose.

NO WRONG TURNINGS

We strolled the path, your two steps to mine,
with the Labrador who strained at his end

of the leash. He was not willful
but wanting to know the rustle

of tall grass, half-hidden,
his snuffles rich with pollen

and the scent of something wildly alive,
a sudden burst freezing at the edge of his sight.

I stood between holding him back
and leading you on, wanting to protect

the song sparrow whose white throat trilled
for a mate, or the baby rabbit too soon a morsel of two bites.

But you wanted what you saw: the dog's
cocked ears, the tremor of his hindquarters,

the toes digging into the earth preparing for flight.
Your fingers in my hand twisted away: dismissive, reaching.

STEELHEAD FISHING

Wader-deep in the Cedar River,
the man casts his line with a snap of his wrist,
eyeing the hook's descent, the plop,
the moment the silver flash is swallowed
by the current. The road, the hawk's cry,
the wind seem far away or still.
The puffs of his breath are a Morse code:
November almost freezing.

                            Behind him lie
his trampled footprints in mud
as he stepped past the steaming cow pies
from the patched black and white Holsteins,
the farmer's permission. No radio on
in the car as he drove the highway
to Kent, parking by the boarded-up
factory, sign swinging on one nail.

Rain strikes a steady beat,
a song on his slicker and his hood
until the strands of his exposed hair stream.
When was he asked, and who asked him:
What's been the best day of your life?

LATE NIGHT PHONE CALL

I'm grading essays
when the phone rings.
The answering machine
picks up and my father's voice
commands like the jerk
on a dog's leash: "Call me." Along
the paper's margins in red ink,
I scribble, "Pronouns. Who?"
    Rubbing circles into
my temples, I think "An old man's
time is always now. He can wait."
An hour later, I dial and listen
to a chain of rings with no answer.
    After two cups of tea, I'm worried.
It's late. A half-moon rises
in the living room window. A star
falls out of the sky.
    I park my car one block up
from my dad's house. No one hears
my footsteps on the cracked driveway.
The building is green during the day.
    A silhouette shifts against the blinds
over the kitchen's sink where a man
might fill his glass with water. Standing by
the front door, I make a phone call—
promising myself my father will
never know that I'm here.

THE FERAL CATS

The uneven curtains widen with light at dawn—
a golden iris staring him awake.
Why does its magnetism pull him down

the stairs? While slippers scuff the floor, he hikes
the waist of his pajamas as he yawns.
Through glass he spies a calico, black smoke

the coiling of her tail. Other half-grown
survivors mew with rheumy eyes. Blue jays
ratchet a call. He grunts: *They want their goddamn*

peanuts! He'd planned to sleep late today.
The cats keep up their high-pitched choir. He thinks
of when his wife lay in the ICU. There is joy

in being needed now. He mixes chunks
of tuna fish with Friskies pellets. A pan
balances in each spread palm. They eat by rank;

big toms first, brushing his legs—unclean
withers, a wildness he can't touch. A tub
lies tipped on muddy ground. Hungry raccoons

have washed their hands. The shadows ebb
to morning sun. Who else will care
for all this life—his thankful, thankless job?

WHAT EVE NEVER SAID TO CAIN

Nine months after my teeth
nibbled the flesh of the fruit,
my belly grew round.
The birth pains began
as muscles I didn't know I had
contracted. Sweat beaded
my forehead with the hard breath
it took to bear down until
you came squalling into this new world,
spotty with blood. You were my first.
Instinct guided your mouth
to my breast. I was innocent
of such pulling and tugging.
Your late night wails, sharp
as a sickle moon, brought me
to your side. So tethered, I learned
to croon false lullabies to save
my sleep. Always, you wanted
more than your share of figs
or lentils, of the circle of my arms calming
your temper. Then Adam gave me
Abel. I was torn again between
such lamb-soft hair
and your dirt-smeared fingers
grubbing in the earth. Abel,
who would lie quiet and listen
to bird song and wind in the trees.
Of course, I favored what I remembered,
what I once had in paradise.

GIFTS

You laugh and say I don't forgive what I
remember—at Christmas time, my first surprise
inside your parents' house. You asked me why
a china teacup made me narrow my eyes

and groan. I saw no effort on your part—
your mother bought it. But the electric
flower boxed in black you thought was smart?
What do I want? Not things. It's not a trick.

My father's gift to me lies in my genes:
longevity. Alone, without a wife,
he seldom smiles. God knows what lives off-screen
within your cells beyond a surgeon's knife.

Old memories are ghosts we walk through.
Your gift to me? Don't die before I do.

TO MY GRAND NEPHEW, JAMES OF THE FUTURE

If I am gone, twenty years from today,
perhaps you'll find this photo,
recognizing your little boy self—
long before legs lengthened
and voice dropped—
not quite believing
the thickness of your lashes
or the swoop of bangs on your forehead.

But who is the woman
who holds you, you might ask:
this matron on the edge of your memory.
Her glasses slip to the tip
of her nose, speckled age spots
glossing a cheek as she reads
and points out the waves
in *Where the Wild Things Are.*
In the boat of her lap,
your straddled calves
rest on the knobs of her knees.
Maybe you'll blink, thinking
that boy can't be you,
while the muscles in your right arm
consider the arc, the heft of a stone
skipped into the bay, hinting at
what I once showed you.

Right now, I'm here to say
you have big ears
like my own grandfather
I sometimes recall. That day
your shoulders leaned back
into me. Warm scent under my chin,
slowly absorbed by the leaf pattern,
I settled and sank into the chair.

THE RIGHT KIND OF SONG

In the room where he knows
he'll spend the rest of his life,
my father sits in a wheelchair.
Today, two volunteers
from a church came to sing
for the seniors, visiting each room.
That's nice, I say
but Dad shakes his head,
They were terrible.
                        I know better
than to ask as he rants: *No Perry Como*
or even Dean Martin with words
that people here know. His lips
mash down tight, eyes turned
towards the window where January
rain tatters the bark on the trees.

My father used to sing.
With each bounce
of his knee, his hands held
a childish me steady. The years
swirl and now I listen
to that alto voice sing along
to the Andrews Sisters
of how *one night*
when the moon was so mellow,
Rosita met young Manuelo
to each of my sister's girls.

The sounds come back
like separate notes thrumming
up my throat, over my tongue.
Ti-pi-ti-pi-tin, Ti-pi-tin, I sing.
The corners of Dad's mouth begin to lift.
Outside, the rain drums.
I take a deep breath
to repeat the chorus.

LAST DAY

I try so hard to stay awake—head up,
then down with chin on chest. From far away
I hear a voice I lost: *Is he asleep?*
In her black skirt and heels, all fuzzy, I see

my daughter come from work. But why she speak
like fancy doctor? Secrets. Sneaky cancer.
No pain—just quiet like great big snowflake
snuffing me out. It ninety years so far.

Strange dream I have. Maybe I lose my mind.
The newspaper headline say I already dead
but daughter's hands feel warm. Not understand
how can I be this way; I know my blood

go round and round. My heart get tired. Not sad,
just big surprise. Don't fuss for me. No need.

IN FLOWER

After the promise of buds
breaking open, the burst
of color edging the green
comes the full-bodied blossom
and the scent hanging heavy
in the air. There's no turning back
from the wilt, the yellow edge,
the heavy dust of pollen,
and petals let loose from the stem.

PART IV: THOSE LEFT TO TELL

IN HAWAI'I, WE DO THIS

No one wanted to
hold my hand at Brighton Elementary
when the wart appeared at the base
of my ring finger. It was lumpy with ridges
like the barnacles speckling
ocean stones. I wore bow-tied dresses
with pockets, keeping my fist closed.
And under pressure, in the damp heat
of my fingers, the wart dug in and grew.

The doctor's glowing punk
couldn't burn hot or deep enough. Maybe Dad
saw that I believed more in frog spit
and the harsh words of my friends.
In Hawai'i, my father said, *we do this*
and his knife split the eggplant. Two tear shapes
fell to the sides. Dad rubbed the juice
into my hand. Then I followed him
to the far corner of our backyard
where the day seemed dim. No one
would believe me, I thought, as we buried
the eggplant. I smelled the earth
as Dad's shovel tamped it down. He nodded
with the rhythm of his words: *When this rots,*
your wart will die and fall off. All the way
back in to dinner, he held my sticky hand.

THE GOLFER'S DAUGHTER

Herman the mouse skitters
into his living room hole
on our black and white TV.
I'm sipping grape juice

from a plastic cup
when my father strides in
with a golf club nested against
his shoulder. Four mice

in suspenders bend over,
squealing their high-pitched
laughs. *Will you watch me,*
Dad asks, flexing his arms

and planting his feet
eighteen inches apart. Just as
a cat's claws surround Herman,
I nod yes. Dad's fingers

choke down the rubber handle:
Tell me if I move my head.
Herman blinks his eyes,
only his chin and huge ears

are in sight but I'm sure
he'll escape. Over and over,
in swift arcs that scuff
the rug, skimming close

to the ceiling, my father swings.
I know he keeps his jaw down,
anchored to his chest. He won't
see that my eyes haven't left the screen.

ON HEARING OF A FRIEND'S
ONSET OF ALZHEIMER'S

Not now, or tomorrow—
but some day. Each sunrise

and sunset in August gives up
a few minutes of summer

like the Himalayan vine, shriveling,
thorns following the cane

down to the pale
five-petal blossom, the stubborn fruit

ripening to blackberry.
How the tongue

relishes the taste.

HARD SHELL CLAMMING

All day, we bent beside barnacled tide pools,
waves ebbing before Dad's shovel.
As the blade bit the cobblestone beach,
Dad bellowed—battling with the long-handled
burden, a grunt bullied from his belly.
We scrambled for bivalves: little necks,
cockles, baby horse clams. Above us,
a bittern bleated. Bursts of sea water jetted
from blue-tinted shells that hadn't burrowed
deep enough. How the buckets rattled
and banged with each bank shot and blow
of another clam. Dad's battery of pebbles
and water scrubbed out our basin while the sun
bronzed the back of our necks, sand rubbing
between rubber boots and the bare skin
of our legs, but we didn't blanch or slow.
In the bowl of the hole, we bragged about
bingeing on butter and braziers, the boiling
bisques of our labor. No barbs or bickering
between us, we bumped shoulders together
becoming a buttress of siblings—bedraggled
but busy for this bipedal familial business.

SCIURUS GRISEUS

We hear a clatter, a rattle
of toes scrambling the bark
of a hazel wood tree. Then the pitch
of shells striking the deck. I charge

the sliding glass door, rapping
my knuckles and yelling through
the screen. When I turn my back,
they're nibbling my budding nasturtiums,

the gray flags of their tails twitching
a code for dinner. I grit my teeth,
forgetting the time when I scattered
acorns like a farmer casting seeds

from a shoulder-slung bag or the grooves
they gnawed at the wooden box,
frozen shut with snow and twenty degrees—
the smell of peanuts permeating

the air. Just out of reach, they pause
to scratch fleas from their fur, chitter
their animal laugh, and dance from foot
to foot. When I lunge for the door,

they're already running. Their weight seesaws
the limb, bending it like a bow to shoot
gray blurs through the trees, arms and legs
spread as if to grab the arc of their flight.

ARGUMENT ON THE BEACH, VASHON ISLAND

As the low tide curled away
from the barnacles, anemones, red-orange
starfish layered on rock—you seamed
your lips together, glaring past
whatever my finger pointed out
as if to say, *I can see for myself.*
Clam holes spurted sea water
into our pant legs. We branched apart
passing heavy logs of driftwood
settled deep into the sand.
Under the noonday sun, I said nothing
about the reddened back of your neck,
the blush reaching up into your hair.

THEODOR JACOBSEN OBSERVATORY
University of Washington

Too much lamplight in the parking lot
from moving vehicles dims the stars

rising above the cityscape of condominiums
and shopping malls. We fit one eye

to the telescope, to view the rings of Saturn
tilting out of view and the summer

triangle of Vega, Altair and Deneb—
so near, so far.

Our feet feel rooted to this earth
and we are spinning in space. What invisible

energies hold us together: Big Bang, Big Crunch,
Big Chill? Each night we stare into space,

witness the pinprick points of the past
just arriving.

THE BUS DRIVER'S WIFE

A water glass, his socks, the shirt he shirked—
her hands pick up the route he's slowly thrown
around. She knows he hates the weeks he worked

the stop-to-stop people he drove to town,
their sad sack tales of why they can't pay fares,
the stream of copper pennies rolling down

the nowhere aisle. To fill his emptied core,
he swears: *God damn, fuck this.* But then he sees
her slump against the door, how words can pare

away her skin into such raw debris.
Not mad at you, he says. *Just mad.* So lost
in red coronas he can't pry free.

THE GUEST BEDROOM

The tabby flicks his tail
against the white nightgown,
head-bumping her legs, meowing
his distress at the stranger
sleeping behind the closed door
upstairs. She shushes the cat,
filling a glass at the faucet,
watching the water roil.
Standing bare-footed, she sips
and listens hard for a creak
or soft snore, imagines clean sheets
yielding to the weight of a body
on a bed, the pattern of hair
on a pillow. Because the cat
wants her lap, she sits in the kitchen—
the chair's four legs stepping
on moonlight. Her hands slowly
stroke the rumbling fur, the warmth
of its belly and breath.

AT THE FOUL WEATHER BLUFF PRESERVE

Ground fog hangs over the water
of Puget Sound as we emerge
out of alders to advance on the beach.
The two-prong tracks of deer
lie before us like stringed beads leading
away. Our sneakers skitter on slippery
stones, eyes examining the sea wrack
tangled from tidal zones: oyster shells
fused together, cockle shells that shatter
like china plates beneath our weight,
skeletons of sand dollars smaller than nickels.

        The stiller we stand,
the more we can see—so many baby white crabs.
Then a clatter, a rattling trill, and a kingfisher
dives low, warning us. The returning tide
freshens anemones and colonies of clams
as the sky clears to blue so bright,
we shade our eyes with hands scratched by sand,
full of what the sea has left behind.

BADMINTON

It's dusk. The shadow branches
of the plum tree inch
their way across our backyard,
lightly touching the badminton net

strung across the lawn. Mom,
my big brother and the baby girl
of our family against Dad
and me. I extend my arm,

feeling the stretch from my shoulder
all the way down to where the fingers
grip the racket and there's a sweet
bounce of strings connecting

with the rubber-nosed birdy.
My father shouts, "Good one!"
as the arc of its flight sails
into the air. He's half-stumbling

in the rutted grass when a wild wave
from my brother arrows a return
over my head into my dad's
backhand. The sun dips below

the horizon but with the ping
of an overhead shot and a near
miss scrapes the wood, still the birdy
is flying. And no one is counting

up points, just volleys, keeping
the game alive like a clock's steady
pendulum, swinging back and forth
as we all yell "fourteen, fifteen,

sixteen," years before a sibling's
divorce, the millennium, the inevitable
death of both parents. We don't know
how happy we are. In the fading

red afterglow, our family keeps playing.

THOSE LEFT TO TELL: FOR A. C.

The Igbo of Nigeria believe
you're only gone when the last relative

who remembers you has died. Dear cousin,
we're old enough to recall Grandma's kitchen—

the Nehi bottles of orange fizz lined up
for special meals on New Year's with the shrimp,

those stiff translucent shells we snapped in half.
Her sink was wide and deep—big enough

to wash my sister in. Fifty years:
the largest anniversary picture

barely held us all while our numbers
quickly spread like ripples fanning far

from shore. Only Aunty Meri
lives on; my mom, your dad—a fading story

that holds huge holes we'll never fully know.
Memory makes of us brief cameos.

Sharon Hashimoto's first book of poetry, *The Crane Wife* (co-winner of the 2003 Nicholas Roerich Prize and published by Story Line Press), has recently been reprinted by Red Hen Press. Her work has appeared in *American Fiction, The American Scholar, Barrow Street, Louisiana Literature, North American Review, Poetry, Prairie Schooner, River Styx, Shenandoah,* and other literary publications. She is a recipient of a N.E.A. fellowship in poetry. Recently retired from Highline College after twenty-nine years of teaching, she writes poetry, short stories, and is currently at work on a novel.